Mad, Bitter, Angry, Saved, Hurt, & Restored

LaVonda Rita Campbell

WestBow
PRESS
A DIVISION OF THOMAS NELSON

WestBow Press books may be ordered through booksellers or by contacting:

WestBow Press
A Division of Thomas Nelson
1663 Liberty Drive
Bloomington, IN 47403
www.westbowpress.com
1-(866) 928-1240

ISBN: 978-1-4497-4487-8 (sc)
ISBN: 978-1-4497-4488-5 (hc)
ISBN: 978-1-4497-4486-1 (e)

Library of Congress Control Number: 2012905789

Printed in the United States of America

WestBow Press rev. date: 4/6/2012

CONTENTS

DEDICATION

"Dedicated to the Memory of my loving husband Albert Louis Campbell and the greatest loving grandmother in the whole world Josephine Stinson. *"GONE BUT NOT FORGOTTEN! I LOVE YOU, ALWAYS!*

ACKNOWLEDGMENTS

First, I would like to thank the Lord for His mercy and grace and for allowing me to go through and come out of all my trials and tribulations victoriously. He has kept me in my right mind.

I would like to thank my mom, **Porchia Reed**, for everything she has endured, learned along the way, and become so that we could have the relationship that we have now. I love you, Mom!

Additionally, I would like to thank my former pastor and first lady, A. W. and Lillie Pope, for all their love and patience with me and allowing me to call them at all times of night, worrying them. I love you.

To Carla Pope-Green, I love you for being there for me and being real in my life. I thank God for my friend, Melisa Miller, who was there when I needed her.

I thank God for my present Bishop and first lady, J. W. and Helen Bracy, for their love and encouragement. Thank you for pushing me into my calling as well as not letting me sit down on the gifts God placed in me. I love you.

To my children, Apree Jamiya Jackson, Dominique Porchia Campbell, Qwaunze Kaliq Campbell, and Denzel Jamal Davis—thank you all for weathering the storms with me and being obedient. Thank you for your unconditional love. Just know I only want the best for each of you.

Thanks to all the other people who caused me drama, pain, and suffering. You all helped me to love harder, learn how to look beyond negativity, and grow spiritually in God. I truly love you all. I thank God for the seasonal people He placed in my life to help me learn the difference between real and fake friends.

To the men who have come in my life and left my life—thank you for whatever role you played, whether good or bad. My prayer for each of you is that you are blessed and see my dust as I go and grow stronger. Please don't get upset if you don't see your name. The page isn't long enough. God bless each one of you.

CHAPTER 1

INNOCENCE TAKEN

I grew up in what was considered the good housing projects in Memphis, and it was much better than the rough areas. In our neighborhood we had a playground and a lot of children to play with, and our days were filled with laughter. As a child at the age of ten, having fun was all I knew, since most of our parents went out a lot or had boyfriends that we did not like.

When I was eight years old, I was molested, but I did not know what was happening to me. I heard girls talking about things that happened and why some of them were living with grandmothers or aunts. Then I realized what had been happening to me.

My mom had a boyfriend who lived with us, and I did not like him. He used to look at me in ways that made me feel very uncomfortable and said little things to me that I knew he should not be saying. He would touch me in places I knew he shouldn't. I told my mother about it, and because she knew we didn't like him, her response was that we just did not want her to be happy. Those words pierced my heart. I was mad that she did not listen to me. Because my mother didn't say anything to her boyfriend, he felt like he could continue doing what he was doing.

Some nights, my mom's boyfriend would come home drunk after disc jockeying. He would come into my room, touching me all over. I would lie there and cry, feeling vulnerable and scared, because I had no one to tell—not even my own mom. He continued molesting me for about three months before he finally raped me one night when my mom and aunts were at a club. I lay there, crying and hurting, wishing that I could die or that my mom would have listened to me. I knew that she would not believe me if I told her what he had done. Her words were imbedded in my head.

It made me angry, and a part of me felt lost and taken advantage of. I had become a child scorned for life. I wanted to kill the man who hurt me; I wanted him dead. I didn't really know what prayer was or how to pray, but I remember asking God to make it stop and saying I wish this man were dead. Two weeks later, he was killed in a motorcycle accident on his way home from playing at a club in Mississippi. To me it was justice, and I did not shed one tear. That anger and hurt stayed buried inside of me. My mom and I were never close after that. Her refusal to defend me had driven a wedge between us, and from that moment on, I never trusted another man. I had become an angry, bitter child. I lived my life in a kind of fear that no child should ever have to live in.

Two years passed, and along came another live-in boyfriend who was worse than the other. In the beginning, he was all right, but once he and my mother got married, the saga began. He drank a lot, stayed out all night, came home angry, beat my mom, found reasons to threaten us, cheated, and everything else under the sun. My brother, sisters, and I would lie in bed, angry, crying, afraid, and hurt, knowing that there was nothing that we could do about it. We feared that a he would pull a gun on us as he had done before. We had to hear the agony of our mom being treated like a child. We were being provoked to anger, and it hurt like hell.

Colossians 3:21says, "Fathers, provoke not your children to anger, lest they be discouraged." So I say to you parents—because there are some men, boys, women, and girls who are being abused—if you are in an abusive relationship or environment, for the love of the children and their sanity, get out! Abuse is not love.

Love is not abusive or violent; it does not hurt. It does not matter if the abuse is physical, emotional, or mental; emotional and mental abuse can be just as painful and damaging as physical abuse. If someone loves you, he or she does not hurt you. Colossians 3:19 says, "Husbands, love your wives, and be not bitter against them."

Ephesians 5:28 says, "So ought men to love their wives as their own bodies. He that loveth his wife loveth himself." This goes for wives as well. Do not allow yourselves to continue believing that you deserve to be abused or that because you saw your loved one being treated that way, it is right. Abuse is not right or okay; it is time for you to bind generational curses (family problems that pass down). Do not allow generational curses to continue; they could cause your life or your child's life. If you do not put a stop to the abuse, you will continue allowing your past to rob you of your future.

Do not be afraid to start over; trust God to open doors, make ways, and be your provider as only he can. Continuing to allow yourself to stay in abusive situations will provoke you to be angry and bitter; just trust God enough to lead you out of the abusive situation. Love yourself enough to know that you and your children deserve better.

I wish my mom would have taken action. I think that if my mother had been stronger and stood up to her abuser, she could have helped us and been there when we needed her. The very man we watched abuse our mom raped me. Because I remembered what I was told the first time, I was afraid to tell my mom. Since he knew that nothing would be done, he continued abusing me. Eventually, I got tired of it and ran away, leaving my sisters behind to face the same abuse. I was told that my sisters were raped and reported it; they were removed from the home and placed in foster care.

Our stepfather was brought up on charges. I was asked to testify that my sisters were making it up. Even though my mom did not help me or listen to me when I needed her, I still loved her and did what she asked of me. I pray every day that God will heal my family and set them free from bondage.

Parents, these are the things that happen when you are so entangled in your own lives that you do not pay attention or listen to your children. Never put children in a compromising position where they have to choose; you will damage them for life, especially if they never find God. The girls will be so damaged that when decent men come along in their adult lives, they will not know how to keep or receive real love for fear of being hurt.

I used to be like that. After I was kicked out of school, I went to live with my aunt in the real public housing projects. I never said anything for fear that no one would believe me or that it would get back to my mother. While staying with my aunt during the last few months of my senior year in high school, a major, life-changing experience took place. I was standing outside the gate of my aunt's apartment, talking to my brother about his plans for his wife's birthday later that evening. After I finished talking to my brother, he pulled off. I began to walk inside the gate, and suddenly, I was snatched into a car through the window. It was not hard, because I was a small-framed young lady.

There were three guys in the car—two in the front and one in the back. They sped off down the driveway with me in the car. The car smelled like marijuana. As they were driving, the one in the back began touching me, and I began to push his hands off me. He began to beat me and forced me to drink some kind of alcohol. He drugged me by jabbing a needle in my arm. Then they all raped me, leaving me lying in the woods for dead.

But God was not ready for me to die yet! I asked, "God, what have I done to deserve the things that were constantly happening to me?" As a child, how was I supposed to believe in God when he allowed such things to happen to me repeatedly? I lost my faith and belief in God. After that, as far as I was concerned, nothing and no one mattered to me anymore. I had begun to let life be all about me and what I wanted. I felt alone and trapped in the housing projects, and I lost hope.

CHAPTER 2

IT IS ALL ABOUT ME NOW!

After that incident, it was hard for me to try to finish high school. I attended three high schools my senior year. I went buck wild. I was very smart, but I began making stupid decisions. I was beginning to let life be about what I wanted.

I began hanging out with a big-time drug dealer. He was giving me the world—or so I thought. I was almost seventeen when I met him. The way he handled business was so fascinating that I watched every move and transaction. I got all the knowledge I could about the game. I started getting my schoolwork from my teachers early so I could turn in my assignments and then cut school to hang out with him and travel. We went to Michigan, Florida, Chicago, and wherever else needed to make our drug pickups and drop-offs. I loved driving down to Florida to make pickups, because I got to do a lot of shopping before I caught the bus back to Memphis with the pickup.

The police and drug dogs were hot in Florida during the summer, so I had to get the drugs and bring them back on the bus. When I would get back to Memphis, I would get off at our meeting point, make my drop, and go shopping.

It was all about me and mine; I did not care about anything or anyone else. I had been violated, so why should I care about anything or anyone else?

I was all about making money, shopping, and fighting—just to forget about what had happened to me. I had become bitter with the world. I turned to gangs to fill the voids only to become more violent and hateful. I dared anyone to approach me the wrong way.

I met another other guy who seemed to be a bigger drug dealer than the guy I was with. He was sexy, fine, handsome, and a smooth talker, too; he possessed all the qualities to trap a hurt, broken, mad, bitter teenager looking for everything she felt she was missing in all the wrong places. I became so fascinated that I thought I was in love and moved to New York with him.

When we got to New York, everything was great for a minute—that is, until I met the other women. I found out that he was a drug dealer and a pimp. He was a con and a master manipulator. He talked me into working for him. Since I had no feelings after everything that had happened to me, it did not bother me. I had a great penthouse with no worries until something happened that changed my whole life.

I got caught up with the wrong people again, but this time, the situation was very scary. I was a long way from home with no family and only my boyfriend to depend on. I had gotten pregnant, was arrested, and was sentenced to life in prison without the possibility of parole being in the wrong place with the wrong people at the wrong time,—and he left me hanging. Too ashamed to contact my family, I had to suffer, because this was a part of my life that I dared not tell anyone. It was going to my grave with me.

One of my johns found out about my arrest and came to help me. He was one of the ones who did not want to sleep with me; he just always wanted to talk. By the way, he was a doctor. He hired a lawyer to help me. While I was incarcerated, there was a girl who kept coming to me, trying to get me to read the Bible and talk about God. I kept telling her she had better get out of my face before I killed her, but she was persistent. She took the beatings I gave her. I was put in solitary confinement every time I beat her. This went on for about three weeks, which meant my john could not visit me.

I was very upset to the point that I wanted to kill that girl. She was interfering with the only help I had in New York with no strings attached. The second time I came out of confinement, the girl came to me again, telling me God loved me and wanted to save me. I laughed at her and said, "If God is real and loved me, why am I in here for something I did not do, and why did He allow all this stuff to happen to me? Girl, if you do not get out of my face, I am going back to solitary, and I mean it!"

The girl kept talking. I pounced on her again and wound up back in solitary confinement after being out for only one day. I was in confinement for a whole week. When I came out, my cell was open, and there was a Bible opened up on my bed to Psalm 37. I was mad. My door should not have been opened, and the guards should not have allowed anyone in. I did not know I was being set up by God.

I called the jailer and asked why my door was open and where the girl was, because I knew she had put that Bible in my cell. The jailer looked at me like I was crazy. She said, "Your cell was not open" and acted like I had not just got of solitary. I asked her where the girl was, and again, she acted as if she did not know what I was talking about or who the girl was. It was as if the girl did not exist.

I turned, went back to my cell, and began staring at the Bible on my bed. I knew something was not right, so I picked it up bitterly and glimpsed at it. I began to read the words, "Fret not thyself because of evildoers." That got my attention, so I continued reading. As I sat there, reading those words, tears began to well up in my eyes. I did not know why, but I began to feel hurt. I lay down on my bed, and then I heard my name called for a visit.

My visitor was the john. He told me that the lawyer got a new trial and would help with the adoption of my baby. I had my baby, but I did not want to see my baby, because I knew it would have been hard to give it up. I had sense enough to know I should not bring a child into my corrupted life.

Two weeks later, the ruling was overturned, and I was given credit for time served. I was very excited. God sent a guardian angel to get my attention while He had me in a place where I could not move. I was being set up for the beginning of my transformation, and I did not even know it.

Young people and parents should read 1 Timothy 6:10, which says, "For the love of money is a root of all kinds of evil. Some people, eager for money, have wandered from the faith and pierced themselves with many griefs" (NIV). Philippians 4:6 tells us to be careful for nothing. Therefore, I am telling you to love yourself and your family more than money or anything it can buy. Hear what I am saying now before it is too late; to learn a lesson the way I did is not worth it.

Parents, when your children start acting out in a manner such as I did, trust that they are dealing with a battle within; you have to get to the root of it. Force them to talk to you, but in a loving way. Let them know that they can talk to you and that you will *listen* to them. If you do not listen, be prepared to see what I became enter into your home. Do not be so holy or self-centered that you do not know how to love your child or identify changes in your child.

Sometimes you may have to use tough love if the situation has gotten out of hand. When you do not back down, you will save your child's life. Do not allow friends, family, or your children tell you that you are wrong or are being too hard. Stick to your guard, and you will see that it is working for the good of your children.

Romans 8:28 says, "And we know that all things work together for good to them that love God, to them who are the called according to his purpose." There is a plan and a purpose. You do not want your child to suffer like me. What I did not say yet was how God spared my life in spite of myself. I was still hardheaded and rough even after I was released from prison and returned home. I just kept running back to my vomit. Oh, yes! God did not spare my life one time, but three times. I say my life was saved once for the

Father, once for the Son, and once for the Holy Ghost. I was so out there.

I was in a car accident on October 31, 1989 at 10:39 p.m. on my way to a Halloween party with my boyfriend. I was sharp from head to toe and sexy, too; you could not tell me anything. A seventeen-year-old had taken his father's truck without permission, drove across four lanes on Shelby Drive, and hit us on the driver's side, knocking my side into a concrete pole. My boyfriend only got a rip in his pants leg with a minor cut, but the seat was folded over me, and my head went through the windshield.

The accident responders had to use the Jaws of Life to get me out. All I can remember before I went into a coma was begging the paramedics not to cut my dress. I was telling them that there was a zipper on the side, and they were telling me they could not move me. I kept insisting that they not cut my dress. I had flown to New York just to buy that dress so no one else would be dressed like me. I was so materialistic and self-absorbed that I was lying there, half-dead, worrying about a dress because I flew out of town to get it.

As I lay in a coma, I saw my spirit outside of my body, looking down at it. My mom, grandmother, and boyfriend were sitting around the bed, crying. I asked them, "Why are you crying?" but I got no response. I tried to reach out to them, and my hands went through them. It scared me badly! There appeared a little angel and a little devil—one on each shoulder—like there was a war over my soul and whether I died or lived. The angel was bidding me to change my life, and the devil was telling me God was going to kill me anyway. The devil said I should not cry, plead for forgiveness, or repent, because it will not do me any good.

Apparently, God forgave me and gave me another chance, because I am still here. When I woke, I found my family, the firefighters, and the paramedics around me, telling me about myself. I was told about all the internal injuries and bleeding that I had and that the doctors were afraid to operate on me or move me, so they let me hold my own. I was taken off life support and pronounced dead, but I am still here. Prayer changes things! The people at the hospital called me my mom's miracle child until the day Baptist Hospital on Union closed its doors. They had never seen anything like my recovery.

The Bible lets us know that God specializes in things that seem impossible to man. James 5:16 says, "The effectual fervent prayer of the righteous man availeth much." That let me know that someone was praying for me, because I definitely was not praying for myself. The strange part about the whole situation was that when the doctors gave up on me, my mom was telling them that she refused to believe it, because I was a fighter, and I would not give up on life like that. No matter what your situation, circumstance, or what the doctors say, just know God is in total control of every aspect of your life.

After I got out the hospital, I went right back to the same old fast life I was living in spite of what I had been through and God giving me another chance to get it right. I continued to be ignorant. The third time God spared my life, I was in a drive-by shooting. As usual, I had to be the bad, bold one. I watched my friend get shot and killed. I got so angry that I grabbed her gun and mine. I got out of the car while bullets were spraying and started shooting. I was shot in the leg. I was lucky, because I could have been killed with all the bullets flying.

I could not go to the hospital, because I did not want to go to jail. One of the gang leaders took some whiskey and a knife to remove the bullet; the scar is still there to remind me of my ignorance. It was another warning that I did not receive about being foolish. Arrogance is not cool, cute, or funny. Give it up! You can have all the money, clothes, and arrogance you want, but these things are not going to replace or fix what is wrong or what you have chosen to bury on the inside. Once I learned that, I really was caught up and lost.

I became a user instead of a dealer who followed someone else. I got so strung out on crack that I lost everything; I almost lost my mind. When I got sick and tired of being sick and tired, I looked at myself one day in the mirror. I did not like what I saw. I immediately began to cry. I was broken to the point that all I could do was cry out to God. I said, "Lord, if you are real, I do not want to be like this anymore."

God delivered me instantly. I have never touched or used drugs again. That prayer was in August of 1989. I did not run to rehab. I knew that rehab could not help me; it would have only been a temporary fix, and I needed a permanent fix that only God could give me. True drug addicts cannot face themselves in the mirror; because they enjoy what they do, they cannot face reality. I want to let you know that rehab is not the answer. That why relapses always occur—it is not the answer; God is!

I have learned that I had warnings in my life and did not know it. Well, I did not understand them. I was so deep in bondage that nothing mattered. Proverbs 16:18 lets me know that "Pride goeth before destruction, and a haughty spirit before a fall." When people come to you to try and help steer you straight or you hear the Word and it convicts you, listen, because you may not get the chance that I got. When the warning comes, evaluate your life and know that the fast life is not worth your life. I did not heed to it the first, second, or third time. I thought everything was all about me, but it was not. I was self-destructing without knowing that there was another plan for my life.

CHAPTER 3

MEETING OF THE SAINTS AND GETTING SAVED

I started back dealing drugs, using them, and prostituting again, because I was dead on the inside. I had been violated, and I buried the anger and bitterness way down deep—as if it never happened. I had made up my mind that I would never love anyone completely or trust anyone. I began to feel worthless and unworthy of being love. My boyfriend knew everything that was going on, but because I had given him a good life, he did not say anything. We were both doing the same mess.

One day, my boyfriend came to me about his mom and asked if she could come live with us. I was not having it! I told him that he had two brothers and a sister. Why she could not go live with them? He loved his mother, and I could not knock him for that—that is, until he told me she was sanctified. I did not know what that was until she got there. She told him that the Lord told her to choose him, and I was very upset.

My boyfriend's mother walked around all day, singing gospel songs, praying, putting oil everywhere, and reading the Bible. She even had the nerve to have the Bible open on my living room table. One day, I just got sick and tired of her. I told my boyfriend that she had to go with all that God stuff. She had started messing with my money, my business, and making my customers nervous. I could not have that. Little did I know it was a *SETUP*.

My boyfriend's mother overheard him and me arguing about her, and she began telling us about our sins—in my house. *Huh*—the nerve of her. She went on and on about how we should not be shacking up and even said she would not leave us alone until we went to church with her. *Ooh!* I was so mad that I could have chewed barbwire. I immediately told him that we were going to church with her that Sunday.

Sunday could not come fast enough for me. I trusted and believed that when my boyfriend and I went to church, his mother would be quiet and stay in her room until we found her someplace to go. I wanted her gone. She disrespected me in my own house. *She had better been glad she is his mother,* I thought to myself.

When we got to church, it was nothing that I was used to. The church was small and smelled like hogs. A little old woman sat in a chair to my left when I came in. She had a spit cup beside her; in my mind, it was disgusting. There was a preacher there who was an evangelist. He was a little man, but if I were not looking at him, I would have thought he was a big man by the way he talked.

People were shouting and yelling all around me. I did not know what they were doing; I thought they had lost their minds. I was just there to get my boyfriend's mom off our backs. Mind you, I knew nothing about the Holy Ghost or sanctification. I must say, though, that little man sounded good—that is, until he called me out. I started looking around to see who he was talking to. Then he said, "I'm talking to you."

Since I was raised to respect my elders, I got up and went down the aisle grudgingly. I could not figure out why the minister was calling me. He began speaking to me. He told me about myself, what I was doing, and how God had spared my life three times. I got angry and started looking around to see if I knew anyone who had told this man all my business. I was ready to fight; little did I know that my whole life was about to change.

The minister scared me so badly when he told me that I had better run for my life that I did not go back to church for two months. At the same time, it was like something had happened to me. I tried to go back to my normal fast life, but I was hindered by something. I could not make money or do the things I used to. I became afraid and began to use drugs more until I became addicted and started prostituting more to keep up my habit. I began to lose everything, because I allowed my boyfriend to keep telling me that the minister wasn't real so I could keep doing what I did. We both had habits, and I did not want to face or deal with the realities of life anymore.

About three months after my boyfriend and I went to church, his mother invited us to go to a revival at that same little old church. I went, but he did not. I did not know what to expect at a revival. When we got there, that same man was doing the revival. He called people out, and they were healed. I thought they were being paid to act like they had been healed.

Two rows in front of me, a grandmother sat with her granddaughter, who had been burned badly from her head to her feet. The pastor told the grandmother to bring the baby down, and God would heal her completely with brand new skin. I knew I had to come back, because that was something I had to see with my own eyes. I did not believe it. A couple days later, she was back with her granddaughter. Lo and behold, that baby had brand new skin like a newborn. I had to look hard to make sure they did not switch the child or that I was not so high that I was seeing things.

Amazed at what I had seen, I went home, not saying anything to my boyfriend. I went into the bathroom and looked at myself—something I had not done in a long time. The next morning, I went in the bathroom again, looked at myself, and knew I wanted a serious change—for real this time. I began to cry. I could hear words that I had never heard before—"with a broken heart and a contrite spirit." Although I did not know what they meant, I began to feel broken. I felt a change beginning to take place in my life. I wanted a real change—not like other people who think that they can bribe God to get him to do what they want and then go back to their old ways.

God knows the heart and your thoughts before they enter your mind, so He already knows what you are going to do. I found myself wondering and wanting to know where this evangelist was, because I wanted to go where he was. I found out where he was, and I went to him. When I got there, I saw people putting down walkers and walking, being healed from medications, and a lot more. I knew I wanted to follow him and get the help I needed to get my life together. I did not want to give up shacking with my boyfriend or my money and get a real job, but I did.

The more I went to church, the more I learned and the more I hungered and thirsted to be right in God's eyes. I knew I wanted the change; whether my boyfriend did or not did not matter. It was not easy at all, but the main thing was to keep going regardless of anything and anyone else.

I joined the Army reserves on the delayed entry program. Shortly after joining, my unit was put on lock down and sent to Desert Storm. I was upset. I was not going to get in anyone else's business; of course, I rebelled and challenged everything the officers said.

While being processed in, I found out I was pregnant. I did not believe it. I made them do the test five times, telling them someone was mixing up my test with someone else's. "Oh my God" was all I could say. I had cheated on my boyfriend a couple times with a jerk in my unit on a bet, since he thought he was all that and a bag of chips. (Whatever.) This man was not really worth my time. I could not believe I was pregnant, because I had been told that I could not have children.

I did not want to be a mother at that time; I did not even know who I was. I told my boyfriend, and he was happy and proud. He asked me to marry him. Two weeks later, I was assigned to another unit, since my permanent unit had gone to Iraq. My unit was assigned to go to Camp Shelby for training. I had to be down there for two weeks with the jerk I cheated with. Seeing him every day and not knowing if my child was his or not was horrid, because I could not stand him. Guys like him make women click out. I knew that if he were my child's dad, my child's life would be messed up. We stayed into it at Camp Shelby. He made me so mad that I tried to blow him up in his truck, until someone stopped me.

My unit left early to come back home. I did not call my boyfriend, because I wanted to surprise him. To my surprise, when I got home, I caught him in my house with someone else. It was not pretty. I beat the crap out of her and threw her clothes over the balcony. Then I went downstairs and busted all the windows out of her car and my boyfriend's. I went to my friend's house and mixed up some sugar, eggs, and Snickers to put in his gas tank.

When I got back, this woman was yelling out her car window, and I punched her in the face again. I tried to snatch her out the window, but she drove off. I went upstairs to deal with my boyfriend. I let him know that I was taking everything, because it was mine. I told him he was lucky that I did not kill him. He was not worth it. Instead of going to jail, I went to my mom's house to cool down.

The next day, I got another apartment. I refused to live with any more unnecessary drama. When my boyfriend got home and saw that I had moved out, he went berserk. He came down to my mom's house, looking for me. My stepdad told him I was sleep. He came in, pulled me off the couch by my feet, and screamed for his ring back. He said the baby was not his, because I left him. I told him that if he did not get his hands off me, I would kill him (but of course, I used some more words). I got loose from him, jumped up, and told him I would give him to the count of three to get out my mom's house.

My mom had some hot water boiling on the stove for her roast. I grabbed that pot, and he began yelling, "You better not throw that water on me."

I asked, "Why are you still here?" Before he could get downstairs, I threw the water on him over the balcony, and he fell down the stairs. He wound up going to the emergency room, but he learned not to ever put his hands on me again.

I went on about my business and did not deal with him anymore. He called, but I did not think about him. I did not care if he was the father of my baby or not. He was stupid, and the other man was ignorant and a jerk, so I did not care if either one was involved or not. I did know that I was a strong black woman. I could stand on my own after all that I had been through.

I knew that I had to find the church where the preacher was so I could get myself together and get back in line before I wound up in jail again—especially after what he had said to me during the revival. I knew this preacher was not like other preachers who had tried to sleep with me or bribe me to have sex with them. Their actions drew me away from church. This preacher drew me in with love and kindness, no matter what my mess. I was never judged. He called and checked on me—he loved me!

Although I was going to church, I feared caring, loving, or trusting anyone because of all the pain and hurt I had buried in me. When I met the preacher's wife and daughter, the love they showed was unbelievable; I never knew that someone could love me. His wife carried herself in a manner where her light shined through hurt, pain, or anything she was dealing with; she loved God and made me want what she had.

The minister's family members were with me throughout my pregnancy, and they did not throw in my face the fact that I was not married. They tolerated my anger, attitude, and stubbornness without judging me; they loved me. Trust me, I dragged them through pure hell, because I had no heart, love for anyone, or feelings; I was cold, angry, bitter, and hurt.

One thing I learned is that when people really love God and are truly sanctified, they do not judge, back bite, or act uppity; they love unconditionally, just as Jesus did. Who are we to judge or turn away a soul? God may be trying to use us to save someone's life, change someone's life, or even just draw him or her to church while he does the rest. That is how I got off the streets and out the gangs—through love and kindness! My new friends did not try to change me; they left it to God. Prayer changes things.

Matthew 7:1–2 says, "Do not judge, or you too will be judged. For in the same way you judge others, you will be judged, and with the measure you use, it will be measured to you" (NIV). Romans 12:3–4 says, "For by the grace given me I say to every one of you: Do not think of yourself more highly than you ought, but rather think of yourself with sober judgment, in accordance with the measure of faith God has given you. Just as each of us has one body with many members and these members do not all have the same functions (NIV)."

Next time you see someone who is not the person you think he or she should be, check your own salvation. Ask God to show you yourself and help you become who he really wants you to be. We never know what someone has to be delivered from, has been through, or has been delivered from. Allow God to remind you where you came from.

It is time to go back to genuinely being concerned for the whole person—especially his or her soul, not just the pocket. That is how I got my life together—real saints. God will use whoever heeds his voice. No matter what you are going through, allow God to use whomever he puts in your path to help you; you will never know what can or will happen until you do. Regardless of where you have been, what you have done, or where you are in life, God loves you and wants to heal you completely. Walk into your divine purpose, and let God use you. If I can do it, so can you; you have not heard the whole story yet.

Switching sides is definitely not easy. You are going to have a lot of struggles, trouble, trials, tribulations, and most of all, tests. Just know that they are working for you, not against you, not matter how it looks or seems. They are all for growth, testimonies, and strength. You never know when you may have to face one of your demons again, so stay strong, no matter what. If you fall down, get back up. Do not wallow in your mess. Clean yourself up, and keep it moving. Remember this one thing—if you keep your eyes on the prize (getting into heaven), you will succeed in everything you do.

Chapter 4

The Military, Marriage, Separation, the Woman, Back Home, and Divorced

After having my baby, I knew I needed a change of environment. Since I was a new babe in Christ and dealing with demonic spirits, I was struggling with coming out of the life I was in. I joined the Army full time! I did not want to leave my baby, but I knew I had to make a better life for my child. It was very hard.

Me in the Army—*wow*. People laughed and thought it was a joke, but I knew I had to separate myself for a while. I had to gain strength and get some much-needed discipline so that I would be able to face the people in my life who said I would always fail or wind up dead. I wanted to show others something that they would be proud of me doing. I wanted my light to shine before them and stand against the wiles of the enemy that sought to destroy me.

The Bible lets us know that we wrestle not against flesh and blood, but against spiritual wickedness in high places. I refuse to be in bondage to my past or people. I was never a people-pleaser; that is why I knew I had to make a change.

Upon arriving at my basic training site in Fort Jackson, South Carolina, I got a rude awakening that I was not expecting. Fort Jackson was so beautiful compared to

Memphis that I thought I was in hog heaven until the bus pulled up to the reception center. There were a lot of people standing out there in green BDUs (battle dress uniform); at first, they were smiling and talking, so we all figured these were nice people who would welcome us and show us around. We were *wrong!* They were our drill sergeants, and as soon as we got off the bus, they started yelling, "Move it, move it, y'all ain't moving fast enough; get in formation." I knew what formation was, because I had taken ROTC in school and was on the drill team. I must admit that this man's Army was nothing like ROTC.

The drill sergeants acted like they had lost their minds with all the yelling. I said to myself, "Lord, what have I gotten myself into?" I had recently been saved, and I did not think I would be treated like this. I knew it was going to be a long eight weeks.

While in formation, the drill sergeants asked us if anyone had taken ROTC. Like a dummy, I eagerly and happily raised my hand and was appointed platoon guide. At first, I thought it was going to be easy and great—that is, until they asked if anyone knew what the letters in the word "Navy" stood for. None of us knew. They told us it stood for "Never again volunteer yourself." Oh, how true that was.

They marched us over the same day and put us in uniforms. So much for thinking we were going to have free time and wear our civilian clothes for the rest of the week. After getting our uniforms, they marched us over to our barracks, where we would be living. I was upset. I thought since we had all our bags and were then given big duffle bags with all our military clothing in them that we would ride the bus. I was *wrong* again. They marched us with all that stuff, and we could not even help each other carry it. Some girls cried and fell down, and we could not do anything about it. Little did we know that they noted the names of all the girls who cried and fell down.

When we finally made it to our barracks, every one of them was called out and made to get down and do twenty push-ups. I thanked God I made it, because I knew that after marching a half mile with all the bags, I would not have been able to do the push-ups or would have gotten an attitude and not been saved anymore.

After the girls finished doing their push-ups, I was called out with four other girls. I thought, *Lord, what have I done?* The drill sergeants gave us our assignments. The four girls and I were picked as squad leaders, and I had already been appointed platoon guide. After we received our instructions, I was told to stay behind.

Our female drill sergeant let me know that I was responsible for everyone and everything—what was done and not done. I got upset, because these were grown folks. Why did I have to be responsible? I was so mad that I called my pastor and first lady (his wife), because I did not think it was right for me to be responsible for everybody. I thought the female drill sergeant did not like me.

My pastor told me to read Psalms 37 and 34, but my first lady told me, "Nobody told you that the road would be easy; it gets worse before it gets better on this side." I did not like that—not at all. I thought when you were saved, everything would get easier. I thought God would protect me from all hurt, harm, and danger. No, the Bible lets us know that in this walk, we will have trials and tribulation. Hebrews 12:1 lets us know that we have to run the race that is set before us, laying aside every weight that easily besets us (distracts us from doing the will of God for our lives).

I have learned that trials and tribulations work to give us patience, and a patience test is not one you want to ask God for. Be careful when you say, "I do not have any patience." This is from experience, not what I was told. God knew I had no idea what I was asking him for when I got tired of that drill sergeant, exercising, and everything else.

I was told that I had to do a walk-through in the barracks every day after exercising and training with the same female drill sergeant. If someone's bed or job was not right, I had to do push-ups along with everyone except the woman or women who caused the situation. It got old very fast. I was always glad when she was off, because the other two drill sergeants were men, and I felt I had an advantage. They let us talk to the guys in the chow hall and gave us more time to eat.

Our head drill sergeant was a man. Umm did he look and smell good. He was more laid-back—in fact, both men were. Our problems only came from the female sergeant. At one point, she caused me to call my pastor every day. I thank God that I had a pastor and first lady who I could call whenever I needed them. I felt the street in me in rising every time she was on duty. She always found something wrong to make us do push-ups or take away our free time. At one point, I thought I was going to move Fort Jackson to another state with all the push-ups I had to do.

One day, I grew tired of it and stopped calling my pastor, because he kept telling me to read Psalms 34 and 37. I knew our senior drill sergeant was attracted to me, and he was married. What do you think I did? I fell weak to the flesh. Due to temptation, I started smoking again. We were not allowed to have cigarettes, but the senior drill sergeant brought them to me along with other special privileges. Our female sergeant did not like it, but she had to deal with it. I no longer had to do the extra physical training or chores.

I began spending a lot of time with this drill sergeant. Most of the time, he and I went off post when he had to get things for us. We had lunch, romantic days, and great sex. Oh, yes—it went down—trust that it was. It got to a point where he started working seven days a week—including spending the night, just so he could see me and we could spend time together. Of course, the drill sergeants had their own quarters, which was where we were most of the time. We crept all throughout the night, and I got to sleep in late.

After eight weeks of hell (with the exception of my great love affair), basic training was over. Next, we went to our AIT (Advanced Individual Training), where we got our training for our jobs. AIT did not include all the stuff we had to do in basic, and we got weekends off to do what we wanted, but we had to be earn our passes. I was sent to Fort Monmouth, New Jersey—a long way from South Carolina.

I knew I wanted to see my man. Little did I know that I had already gotten him to fall in love—so much so that every weekend, he came to see me and spent the whole weekend with me in New York. He sent me flowers every week; I knew it was wrong, but I needed it—at least, that is what I kept telling myself. You see, basic training included only women, but AIT was coed.

One day, I started getting notes from an admirer. It went on for about two weeks; then I finally responded and asked my admirer to meet me in the basement where we shined our boots and to scratch his head when I walked in so that I would know it was him. Before I went to the basement, I had to call my lover before it got too late. He was on duty in Fort Jackson that night, so I was not going to miss any opportunities that he may have had planned for us. I told my lover about the notes I got and how I was going to meet my admirer to see what he was talking about.

Boy, did he blow a fuse! He started telling me that he was going to leave his wife and be stationed where I was going after AIT. Although I sinned and was in a backslidden stage, God still loved me; I thought He did not, but He did. God immediately brought to my awareness that if this man would leave his wife for me, then he would leave me for someone else. I immediately told him that I did not think we should see each other anymore. He got angry.

I hung up the phone and went to the basement to meet my admirer. After all that drama, I knew I had to compose myself first. I did not mean to hurt this man; I just needed to do things the right way and stop all the foolishness. Paul wrote in the Bible that the flesh dies daily. We all will have struggles of the flesh as long as we live in it, but the more we deny giving the flesh what it wants, the more strength and power we gain over the flesh.

As I walked in the basement into the mist of the crowded room where everyone was shining their boots, I looked around and could barely see my admirer scratching his head. This guy was just as short as me. I signaled him so he could come towards me and we could go outside to talk. We talked for about four hours, getting to know each other. In that time, he decided he wanted me to be his girl.

When my admirer asked me to be his girl, I immediately told him about my former lover. He was shocked and tried to figure it out. I accepted his offer to be his girlfriend. As soon as I did, we got caught by the drill sergeant on duty for being outside after hours. Luckily for us, we were just yelled at and sent to our rooms. The next day, the same drill sergeant who caught us saw us and made us drop (do push-ups). I was happy and mad at the same time.

The weekend came, and my new boyfriend and I made plans to go to New York to see his family. Oh my God! As we were leaving, I could not believe my eyes. We saw my ex-lover on post, and he was not smiling. He approached me with a sarcastic attitude and wanted to know why I just ended our relationship when he was willing to leave his wife.

I told my ex that if he would leave his wife for me, then he would leave me for someone else. He was looking at me as though he wanted to hit my new guy, and I told him to just let it go. He was so angry off that I thought he was going to just click out on both of us, especially when he started cursing, going on about how much he loved me, and asking me what did I do to him.

My boyfriend and I turned and walked away so that we would not miss our train. I could feel the worry from my boyfriend, as if he was thinking, *What have I gotten myself into?* I leaned on him and told him not to worry; I had his back. We laughed it off and got on the train.

We arrived in New York to meet his family. Everyone was great, and from then on, all our weekend passes were spent in New York. We made it through our first month of dating and being stalked by my ex-lover, who finally got the picture and left me alone. I must admit that the four weeks of stalking were miserable, as I tried to move on with my life.

When AIT was finally over and we (my boyfriend and I) were assigned our tour of duty stations, I found out that my boyfriend was going to overseas, and I was going to Virginia. I did not like this; long-distance relationships did not work for me. We put in for a leave of absence, which was granted. During that time, my boyfriend asked me to marry him. I said yes, and we began planning our wedding. At this time, I already had a daughter just over a year old. My boyfriend loved her just like she was his own.

My family and I got everything together for the wedding. Two days before my wedding day, I got a phone call from my fiancé. He got cold feet and decided he did not want to get married. We argued about it; finally, the truth came out. He did not have cold feet. He had a cousin who used his credit cards, and he paid the bills.

This cousin saw her ability to freeload being snatched away right in front of her very eyes. She told my fiancé that she did not like my attitude and I had not done a thing. My fiancé knew we were together the whole time, playing with the baby and having a good time. I confronted this cousin, because I wanted to know what the problem was. Like, I thought there was no problem. She realized that if my fiancé got married, she could not keep using his cards. He would not keep paying the bills; that was a definite no-go.

Sometimes you just have to stand up for yourself and not worry about people. People can mess up everything God has planned for you if you let them. Jealousy will destroy everything and anything—all the time, without fail.

After my boyfriend and I got to the root of the problem, he decided he wanted to go to a justice of the peace in Virginia to get married. We got married, but do not get it twisted—I was upset by all the money that was spent and lost, and I did get it back. Finally, we were married, and he put in a 4187 (a change of duty station request) to change his duty station assignment to Virginia, which is where we wound up.

Life was good at first—until I decided to get out the military when I got pregnant with our first child (my second). I got out and got a job, which my husband did not like, because I made more money than him. Where he came from, women did not make more money than the men. We argued about that, and I tried explaining to him that we were a family. All the money was for our family, so it did not matter who made the most money.

My husband's behavior changed. I knew the signs of a man having an affair, so I did it, too—all over something stupid, and just as I was getting my life back together with God. I spiraled backwards again, into the arms of someone else, because I was rejected over jealousy and money. The Bible is true when it says the love of money is the root of all evil—not the money itself, but the love of it.

Two wrongs do not make a right, so learn early on in your marriage not to take matters in your own hands or do what the other person did to you. Pray without ceasing—no matter what it looks like—do not stop. God will either fix the situation, fix you to deal with the situation, or deliver you from the situation. When God closes a door, do not try to go back through it.

Later, I found out about my husband's indiscretions. I decided not to act like him but do what I should have done first—pray and allow God to work it out. My husband fathered a child only three months younger than ours (as if I had not dealt with that before). My first child's father had a child three months older than mine.

I was sick of the cheating, and through it all, my husband continuously denied the affair and the child. One day, I came home from work, and there was an envelope with a baby's picture on it on my mailbox. I took the envelope off my mailbox and looked at the baby. This child strongly resembled my daughter. The letter ordered my husband to take a DNA test.

I confronted my husband when he came home; again, denial was all I got. I tried to work with him so that the child could be taken care of. He tried to twist things around on me, but I was not going, because I came clean with him about everything I did.

I decided I was not going to live like that anymore. I called my mom and stepdad to come help me move back home. Do not get me wrong—my husband was a great father and husband; the timing was just wrong along with his mentality about money. I moved back to Memphis with my children and forwarded our mail to my mom's address. It took me three weeks to find a job and a place to live after I got home.

I do not believe that parents should raise their children's children except in unfortunate situations. You make your bed; lie in it. When we begin to have children or a family, we should be responsible—whether it works out or not. It is all right if you fall on hard times and need to go home to get on your feet, but do not stay down, expecting your parents to carry you. It is all right to start over, but do not allow yourself to get depressed and stay there. When you do that, then that is the mentality you are putting in your children's mind. Your children will mimic what they see and are taught.

Dust yourself off, and go for the gold; women and men start over every day. You are not an exception; you are just afraid to try or worried about what people are going to say. Well, you need to get over people and realize that your latter will be greater than your beginning. Stop being afraid to fail or start over. Seek God, and put him first. He will direct your path, but he has to be first.

Being back at home was great, with the exception of my job. I had to work different shifts—mostly at night. One night, I was working, and some Caucasian guys came in the store. They started talking, and because I'm friendly, I talked to them. They talked about the money they had lost at the casino. They were mad, and they raped me.

I called the owner of the store and the police, and they just acted as if things like that did not happen in those parts. *Duh!* I should have realized that would be their response, since I was black and working in a small town in Mississippi. Of course, I quit that job. It seemed like history repeated itself, no matter how hard I tried.

After the rape, I started going to the clubs. I just did not care anymore. I felt that even when I tried to live right, I always wound up hurt, mad, bitter, or angry. I was sick of it. Just as I started clubbing and partying, things in my life really took a downward spiral. Thank God for people who prayed for me. I did all that, and it still did not release the pain I felt deep down inside. I felt like I did not fit in anymore.

I realized that once you truly—not halfway, but truly—walk with God and feel His presence, you will not fit in where you used to go or with people you used to hang out with, so there really is no point in trying. The only thing you will do is set yourself up to stay in the valley until you decide to get on the boat. What is the use of doing the same mess and prolonging what you could have or do?

In the midst of getting raped and being wild, I got pregnant. Since I had recently left my husband, I did not know what I was going to do. The guy was wilder than me. He was a stripper that I had dated before and I just did not see a relationship happening, but I knew I had to do something.

I went to see my husband and told him I wanted to work things out. He was getting ready to go overseas. Therefore, we decided that we would and that I would stay in Memphis the year he would be overseas. We made love the whole weekend. That was the plan, anyway—I could not very well tell him what happened to me and what I had done.

Once the weekend was over, I got my children and headed back to Memphis. I did not have an abortion, because I did not believe in them, so I had to make sure that I was in a position where I was able to see and love the child without seeing everything that went on in my life. I still had not settled all the way back down; I was angry all the time while I was pregnant with this baby. I already had two girls, and I waited to find out the sex of my baby. My husband was more anxious than me, and he was overseas.

I finally found out what I was having at seventeen weeks—a boy. My son decided he wanted to come early after I got into a fight. The Red Cross was contacted so they could get my husband home, but he had to wait before he could come home. My baby boy came into this world at twenty-eight weeks, weighing three pounds and eleven ounces. He also had jaundice. He stayed in the hospital for three weeks under a blue light, fighting for his life.

While my son fought for his life, I wished something totally opposite. What I felt in my heart caused me to slip away from God again without even knowing it. I did not know how to love my child; all I could do was keep the secret about him and allow the hurt and anger to continue to grow inside me. I tried to go on living life as though nothing happened, but it did not last.

I treated my son like my daughters to the best of my ability; I thought I had grown to love him. I think the hardest thing for me to wrap my head around concerning my son was the fact that I had surgery and could not understand how I got pregnant in the first place. The doctors told me I had a one in a billion chance of ever getting pregnant.

By the time my son was two, he was always in older people's faces—especially those of women. I thought it was a phase, but it was not; as he got older, it got worse. He never liked to play with children his age, and forcing him to do so made him very irritable. When he was three and four, he was doing things like trying to set the house, the girls' room, and even my room on fire when we were asleep. I brushed it off as another phase.

Parents, that is a big no-no. Never brush off little things—things you think are phases or little things you think are cute are signs that something is wrong. By the time my son was seven or eight, he started getting in trouble at school—bullying children, taking their lunch money, etc. I constantly disciplined him. Although he was afraid of the teacher's calling me, he continued getting in trouble.

One day, I decided to make a doctor's appointment for my son. When the doctor asked me questions about him, I told her about the things my son did. She recommended that I take him to a neurologist. I took him and found out that he had ADHD. If I had not prolonged taking him to the doctor or had not thought the things he did were cute, I could have caught it earlier.

Do not think that your child acting out is cute or be in denial that your child could have a problem. When someone suggests that, do not get an attitude. Do not get mad with people, but get your child checked. The earlier a problem is detected, the better your chances that your child gets treated and lives a normal life without getting into a lot of trouble. God knows I wish I had caught my son's earlier. I had a serious battle on my hands with that boy. All kinds of thoughts ran through my mind concerning him, and they were not good. I paid a price, because I stayed in denial about my child having a problem.

In the midst of dealing with my son's ADHD, I got a phone call one day from my first lady. She said that we needed to talk, so we met at a park near my house. She gave me a word from God. I will continuously say that I thank God for my pastor and first lady. They never judged me but loved me unconditionally.

My first lady let me know that God loved me and wanted to heal me. I had buried hurts that held me back, and I could not grow to my full spiritual potential until I allowed God to close all the doors I had ignored and left opened. When you have been hurt, abused, molested, or raped, you cannot receive what God has for you until you allow him to completely heal and deliver you. That means loving people who hurt you without holding grudges, loving people who spitefully misuse you, and not continuing to let your past rob you of your future. I thought I was healed because I was still going on, but I had blessing-blockers in my way. I had not confronted my bitterness, anger, hurt, or fear of allowing myself to be loved.

My first lady sat there with me, talking and praying until I broke down and allowed God to come in my heart and replace everything in me with forgiveness and love. I told her about everything in my life, and she wondered how I was still sane. This was the same question that I had asked myself.

While talking with my first lady she gave the inspiration that I needed to a new relationship with my mother. I was finally able to see what she had said to me all this time about how she grew up. When you grow up one way, it is all you know, so you tend to do the same things. You have to learn to let go so you can heal, especially if you do not know what another person has been through.

Before we left, my first lady told me to ask God to erase every phone number in my mind that was a part of my past so that I would not keep reaching back to call any of them. Numbers stay in my head, so I asked God to remove them. I also erased them from my phone. Wherever God is trying to place a period or end a chapter in our lives, we have to stop trying to put a comma. We cannot go backward. When God delivered the children out of Egypt, he said, "Do not go back." That means we should not go back to our past, when God is trying to take us forward.

You cannot be truly saved until you are totally delivered. It is time to go forth and be set free. Take your life back, and stop letting the devil rob you of everything you can have—even love. When you go in and out of relationships or allow yourself to be misused, abused, put down, or even raped, you have some barriers that need to be torn down. Only God can tear them down—not other people, psychiatrists, or drugs. Allow yourself to be freed so you can love, be loved, and live. God can take the blinders off, and you can walk into the sunlight of his glory. He's worthy, and so are you. God loves you, and you do not have to be broken.

Once I allowed God to heal and deliver me, I was able to see that my marriage would never be what it could have been. I simply did not know how to truly receive or give love even after everything my husband and I had been through. At the same time, I learned how to love me and live, so I had to let go after the second failed attempt. I decided that I would never date another man as long as I lived. I was to a point where I got sick and tired of dealing with men's drama and heartaches.

I worked as an operator in Georgia for AT&T, which I loved. I especially enjoyed the job's benefits. After sixty days of work, all kinds of benefits were available. People could not wait until their sixty days were up; most got colored contacts and glasses. I also received bonuses.

One evening, I was on my lunch break at work, and a woman came in. I thought she was a man until she started talking. She gave me a strange look and asked me if I brought her something to eat, too. I told her no. Something about the whole scenario that felt completely awkward to me. When I finished my lunch and was on my way back to my desk, I walked past her and said, "I will bring you some tomorrow."

I really did not think anything of the encounter. I just try not act prejudiced towards anyone—or so I thought.

The next day, while I ate lunch, the same woman came in and asked for her food. She laughed, as if I did not have it. I reached down in my bag and got her food. As I raised my head, I saw a look of astonishment on her face. She did not think I had brought it. As I handed her the food, I felt something strange. I thought, *No way; this is not possible. I am not feeling this attraction to this woman just because she is attracted to me.* I shook off the strange feeling and went about my business.

When I got home, I could not rest. For some reason, I could not shake that feeling of attraction towards her. I knew it was against everything I was taught. The next day at work, the woman came over and began talking to me. As she stood there, talking, I got a call for a supervisor, and she took it. I did not know that she was a supervisor.

After the call, she began asking me personal questions. She asked if I was married and if I had a boyfriend. I did not hesitate to answer no. I was shocked at how rapidly I answered. We continued conversing for about a week before she asked me to go on a date with her. At first, I was worried that people would think I was a lesbian, but a part of me did not care what people thought. I went anyway.

About a month after we began talking, she moved in with me. My estranged husband found out, and he was mad. I really did not care how he felt after what he had done to me, but with all the hell and confusion he kept up, I wanted to get out of Georgia. However, in Georgia, I did not have to worry about who knew me. My girlfriend wanted to come to Memphis, but I was a little hesitant about that. I told her I needed to call my folks and give them the heads-up. Some folks asked me if I had lost my mind and if I know my relationship was a sin. Others told me to do whatever made me happy.

As my girlfriend and I got things together to move, my husband popped up at my house with his drama. I had to call the police. We knew then that it was time to hurry up and move. We moved to Memphis, and to my surprise, my mom did not treat her any different than she did us. She accepted my relationship—at least, that was what I felt.

I started going back to my church. For a minute, I would not let my girlfriend come with me. I did not want my relationship to be so obvious. We took trips to North Carolina to see her folks, who were saved. Apparently they accepted her lifestyle, because they loved her, but they did not agree with it. We heard people say over and over that our relationship was a sin and an abomination to God, but no one could show us where it said it was a sin. They just said, "Oh, but it is in the Bible."

After two years of dating, I finally started letting my girlfriend come to church with me. I felt some of the stares, but no one ever said a mean word. The people of the church continued to be loving people. I always told people that I was happy, and I was very happy.

As I began to find my way back to God and grow, something began tugging at me. My girlfriend could feel it, because the same thing happened to her. We did not want to acknowledge it at first, because we loved our happy little family. She was doing everything that a man should do in a relationship. She never spent her money; in fact, she signed the check, and I deposited it in the bank. I paid the bills, shopped for everyone, and whatever else needed to be done. She told me how much she needed for gas, and that was all. She did not have a selfish bone in her body the way most so-called men do.

On our three-year anniversary, my girlfriend and I sat down and decided to pray. We asked God to help us search the Scriptures for ourselves to find out if it really was in the Bible as being a sin for us to be together. We searched and searched. Suddenly we came to Leviticus 20:13.

Let me tell you what the definition of abomination is and where it is derived from. An abomination is a cause of hatred or disgust—a feeling of hatred—and is derived from the Latin word "abominare," which means "to deprecate as an ill omen." Leviticus 20:13 says, "If a man also lie with mankind, as he lieth with a woman, both of them have committed an abomination: they shall surely be put to death; their blood shall be upon them." This includes men and women; there are no gray areas.

After finding this Scripture and reading Leviticus 20, we decided to change our lives and live according to the Word, because neither one of us wanted to go to hell. It was not easy for us to part—in fact, it was one of the hardest things I had to do in my life—but we did. My girlfriend decided to move back to Philadelphia, and I stayed in Memphis and got myself together. I immediately asked God to deliver me from that spirit, and I repented. I was instantly set free from the wiles of the enemy again.

If you are in a spiritual war with homosexuality, do not continue lying to yourself. Do not say you were born that way; it is a lie from the pit of hell. It is another way the devil makes sure he has you lock, stock, and barrel. It is a choice you make, and you have to decide to give it to God completely. Do not allow people to tell you or make you think it is all right, because it is not. You cannot and will not go to heaven as a homosexual.

The Word stands all by itself, and that is why God allows all these things and people to be uncovered. You do not have to stay the way you are; you can be changed. Do not ever think you are hiding your hand, because you are not. God has his people in every place. Do not ever think no one sees or knows, because someone always does. Do not ever think you are in the closet because no one says anything.

God delivered me, and I have never turned back. You cannot let people keep or put you back in bondage when God sets you free. Let them say and think what they want, but he whom the Son (Jesus) sets free is free indeed. Allow God to deliver you, walk forward, and do not look back. You can go on and live a normal, productive life if you allow God to take over.

After I allowed God to heal and deliver me, I decided to turn my separation into a divorce so that I could move forward in my life and make sure no doors were left open. After my divorce was final in 1999, I took some time to really focus on myself—something most people do not do.

As soon as I realized that I was not allowing God to guide me, I remembered what my first lady told me. I had to let everything in my past go. I had to end every chapter God was trying to end and throw the book away so I would not be tempted to read it again.

Many young people—especially women—have to learn to put God first in their lives so that they do not keep winding up with trash. Young ladies, if you focus on God and know that you love yourself, you will not settle for anything less than what God has for you. You will not settle for put-downs, mental or physical abuse, outrage, being controlled, or being made to feel less than what God created you to be. You are a unique, divinely designed woman after God's own heart.

Young ladies, if a man tries to separate you from your family, his intentions toward you are not good. If he's selfish, then he cannot possibly love you or God. If both his things and your things are his, it is a no-go. If he always love you when you have and he needs, it is not love. Take your power back, and gain control over your own life. God will see you through if you seek him.

Men, if you are in the same type of relationship, it is not what God has for you. Do not stay in bondage when God has clearly opened a door of escape. Walk through it, and keep going forward into your destiny. Love does not hurt. It is not puffed up; it is gentle, meek, kind, caring, and concerned.

God knows I love my church, because in spite of everything I went through—even after joining the church— the people at church never judged me. My church was my safety net—my comfort zone. I finally got my life back again. I was restored in God, and my salvation was back on the right track. I allowed God to become the head of my life. I did not want Him to be the co-pilot, which is exactly what He was when I allowed things, people, and circumstances to come before Him.

I have realized that no one ever told me the road would be easy. In fact, I learned that when you truly give your life to God, it gets worse. The devil will not bother you as long as he has you; it is when you decide to change your life. Romans 8:28 lets us know that all things work together for the good of those who love God—those who are the called according to his purpose. When I was saved, I had to learn that the blessings were in the pressing, meaning we have to press toward the mark of the high calling.

When we go through the hard struggles of life—whether they are in marriage, family, finances, or needing self-love—we have to believe and know that we're going through the storm and got to come out without complaining. Many people do not understand that it is so important to not complain while you are in your storm; it only makes the storm last longer. In the midst of all our troubles, we must praise God. When we do so, God will give us a peace that surpasses all understanding.

It is time to forget about folks and what they think and remember the promises of God. In His Word, he lets us know that He will never leave us or forsake us. When the enemy comes in like a flood, the spirit of the Lord will lift up a standard against him.

CHAPTER 5

GETTING MARRIED, BECOMING A PASTOR'S WIFE, AND A BLENDED FAMILY

After getting my life back together, the problems did not end. I thought I finally had peace when God blessed me with a beautiful home in Bartlett. I had no job and made no down payment on the house. My monthly note was cheaper than those of everyone in the neighborhood, and I had a vehicle that was paid for. I continued to praise and magnify God, even with the blessings. Because I did so, He blessed me with a good job.

Since the devil could not tempt me with the things I had always allowed him to anymore, he tried to come at me another way. I went to work one night to find out the company laid everyone off and shut down. I almost started to worry, but I started thanking God for the way being made in advance. People paid my bills without me even knowing or asking; no one knew the need or that I had lost my job, so I knew God stepped in and met the needs.

Unlike most people, I did not call folks to a pity party. People do not understanding that all they are doing is putting up blessing-blockers. When you do that, you doubt God. Without faith (trust), it is impossible to please God. Every person is given a measure of faith, so use it wisely.

A day after God stepped in on everything else, my alternator went out. Normally, I could work on it myself, since I did a little bit of everything, but for some reason, I could not seem to get a particular bolt loose. While I tried to get the bolt loose, my pastor called, needing me to do something. I told him I was trying to fix my vehicle. He started fussing at me, because he was always on me about working on cars, fixing things, and everything else I did that was considered a man's task. He did not want my hands to be rough. He told me to call one of the pastors in our district who was a mechanic. I remembered that I had that same pastor to do some work before, and he was very talkative.

I sighed and wrote down the number with a resentful attitude, because I really did not feel like being on the phone for two hours when calling about one thing. Hesitantly, I called the pastor and told him what my problem was. He started talking to me about everything under the sun except my vehicle. I just listened. He talked so long that my phone started beeping. I told him I needed to call him back because my battery was about to die, and he kept on talking until the phone cut off. I did not even put the phone on the charger right away; I knew he would call right back, and I was tired of talking.

When I put my phone on the charger, it immediately started ringing. The call was from the pastor, and he asked me what happened. *Duh!* I thought. I had told him that the phone was going to cut off. He asked me what time I was coming, and I told him that I would try to drive it over to his house.

When I got to the pastor's house, he started talking, and I thought, *Oh my God! Are you serious?* I immediately interrupted him and asked him how long it would take, because I had to pick up my children from school and cook. Little did I know what was in store for me. He started checking everything except the problem I told him about. He started calling off four or five other problems, one of which was the alternator.

I thought, *Lord, I remember why I never came back to this man before; he talks too much.* One thing was sure—he could not work and talk at the same time. I asked him again how long the repair would take, and he said it would not be long. He told me that I could use his van to do what I needed to do. To me, his offer was a way to make sure I had to come back—and sure enough, it was.

I went to get the children and cook dinner, because I just knew when I got back, the pastor would be finished. When I got there, he was nowhere near being finished—in fact, he had not even started. I was angry. He had the nerve to start talking again and ask me what I was running from. I said, "I am not running from anything; what are you talking about?"

The pastor said, "You running from your calling, and you are my wife." I was so ready to leave when he said that, I felt like my nerves stopped working at that very moment. He came right back and asked me what I wanted to do and said, "We don't have to wait. Let us just go do it—let's elope."

I said, "Um, no, I'm not going to just go do anything. I have to pray. It's been seven years since my divorce." I knew I had asked God for a mate, but he just talked too much for me. When praying, I realized that he talked too much because he did not have anyone to talk to except his girls.

Sunday came, and the pastor was still not finished with my vehicle. I was not a happy camper; I had to use his van to go to church and to our monthly district meeting. To my surprise, when we got to the district meeting, he and I were wearing the same colors. I thought, *Oh, God, what is really going on?* The strangest part was that when he walked up the aisle past me, I felt a strange feeling come over me. I leaned over to my friend and said, "Girl, you ain't going to believe this; that pastor just walked past me, and abnormal feelings came over me. I need to pray." My friend laughed, but I did not think it was funny.

Instead of trying to figure things out, I just allowed God to open my ears so I could hear Him confirm His Word. God will confirm everything He says. After church, I left quickly. I did not want the pastor to hold a conversation with me, because I had things to do. I began to see things that I did not want to see, because I did not want to be married; I was in denial.

God allowed him to keep my vehicle for a reason that I tried not to see, because I did not want to be a pastor's wife. When I realized he was keeping my vehicle so he could see me, I just stopped getting mad; it was not doing any good.

As the week went on and I conversed with the pastor more, I found that I was actually attracted to him and enjoyed his conversation. On the fourth day he had my vehicle (and I had his), I stopped by to see if he had finished. Of course, he had not finished. I told him I was leaving, because I had to get my children and cook. This time, he asked me what I was cooking, and I told him. To my surprise, he asked me to get my children, come to his home, and cook so that the children could meet.

I got my children, and of course, they asked a thousand questions; at this time my children were 11, 12, 13, and 14 and the pastors kids were 12, 14, and 16. Once my children and I got to the pastor's house, the children met each other and went on to have a good time. While the children were inside, the pastor and I were outside. The more we talked, the more comfortable I became with the whole situation. I guess it is true when they say opposites attract, because we were definitely opposite.

As time went by, I began visiting my boyfriend's church on nights that we did not have services. The members at his church seemed nice and welcomed me. The fourth of July came, and we decided to spend it together to see how our children would continue interacting. Although some of the members wanted to intervene, because they were use to planning things for him. We had to let them know what we wanted. That is when he proposed to me again.

My new fiancé set a date for the wedding—September 24. I told him that was not enough time to plan a wedding, and then he said that he just wanted to be married before his annual anniversary as pastor at church. He wanted to have a pastor-and-wife anniversary, not just pastor. I asked him when the anniversary was, and he said it was the last Sunday in October. I did not want to disappoint him, so I changed the wedding date to October 1.

Once we set our date in stone, my fiancé called his eldest daughter, whom I had not met. I had only heard of her, and my fiancé told her about the wedding. She began asking him a lot of questions, but I could not care two cents about any of it. I believed God.

When my fiancé got off the phone, I questioned him, because he seemed upset and told him I did not participate in drama—especially from grown folks with their own families. He told me that his daughter did not run anything; he just wanted her to hear the news from him. Then he began telling me how things were when the girls' mom, his first wife, died.

He said, "Ain't nobody got nothing to say about nothing, 'cause when my wife died, ain't nobody came over here to teach my girls nothing 'bout being a woman, cooked no meals—except for women that was chasing me, and I didn't want none of them. And she wasn't nowhere around when they momma died; in fact, she gave my wife all kinds of hell and drama. She left our home and she winded up getting pregnant at sixteen—she didn't wanna follow the rules." "My wife wasn't having it."

I thought, *Wow! Can we finish planning our wedding now?* (laughing) In the midst of planning our beautiful wedding, I could not help but wonder if the marriage would be the one that would last. I had gotten myself caught before in a so-called second marriage to a man I thought was real, but he wound up having another wife and six children. The marriage was not legal—but that is another book. I have to immediately disregard that whole chapter from my mind and focus on the present.

My fiancé and I got everything together for the wedding with our eight children. There was only one thing that I was not sure about, and that was our honeymoon. I wanted to plan my own honeymoon, but he said he had a woman who was a good friend to his deceased wife who did travel itineraries. I did not feel comfortable with this, but he said, "Trust me"—and of course, I did. She assured us the day before the wedding that everything was set up.

My fiancé and I picked up our Cadillac Escalade, took it to the house, and loaded it up with our things for the honeymoon so we would not have to worry the morning of the wedding. His eldest daughter did not seem to be a problem before the wedding; in fact, we all were at the reception hall, decorating and setting up together. She made sure everything was in place for the reception and cleaned up. The girls and I were spent the night at my house and the guys at his house.

The big day finally came. We all had fun getting dressed; the children seemed to be more anxious than I was. The limousine pulled up. The children and I were at the door before the driver could get out to let us know. I did not want to be late or start late, like most weddings do.

When the children and I made it to the church, it was full. I knew a lot of people there were demonically possessed and did not mean us any good; they just wanted to be noisy or see how it would go. Boy, did I give them something to see with the help of the first lady of the church where our wedding was held. Which is where I worship now.

My first lady (my present first lady) came to the back, where we were, to make sure everything was all right. She asked me if I had a coordinator. I told her no, and she said, "Well, I am going to make sure everything goes well, because there are a lot of people out there that don't mean you any good. Some want to be you, and some want to see you, so you hold your head up, and walk out there real proud. Don't give the enemy anything to talk about."

I replied, "Yes, ma'am." Those words came right on time. God knows what we need every time we need it.

The wedding was great. The reception was perfect, and I did not have to lift a finger. I was very grateful. After the reception, my husband and I got into our Cadillac Escalade and headed for Hot Springs, Arkansas. Halfway to Hot Springs, we stopped and got a hotel room for the night. It was a good thing we did.

The next morning, my husband and I got up early. We were both excited to hurry up and get to Hot Springs. Finally, we arrived at the place my husband's friend had supposedly booked, only to find out that we did not have any reservations. Yes, I was mad—to the point that I could have actually cursed and beaten that woman to a pulp. I turned to my husband and said, "I told you I didn't trust that woman. Now she has our money and won't answer your calls; she must be crazy."

Being the trusting person that he was, all my husband could say was, "I didn't think she would do something like that. What would make a person do such a thing?" I just shook my head and started laughing. Any time people use you to get whatever they want and see another person in the picture or something different, they will try to milk the situation for everything they can.

The Bible tells us to be careful for nothing. I was the one who did not allow people to use me, whereas my husband believed everything people said. I had to protect my husband. I had to help him get to a place where he could see people for who and what they are. Oh, some people did not like it, but I did not care. God gave me my husband, and I was not about to allow people to milk or manipulate him. I knew that others felt like I was blocking their free services and money. The thing is God does not always give us what we want, but what we need.

After calling several places, my husband and I finally found a cabin; we had to have something that would accommodate ten people. We were on our honeymoon for eight days. We spent the first five alone, doing everything from horseback riding to mud baths. My husband was not used to doing any of the things we did, so they were mind-blowing to him.

While on our honeymoon, my husband and I were also in the process of buying a bigger home. Neither of our homes was large enough to accommodate ten people. We had to drive back to Memphis twice to do paperwork for the home that we found. On the fifth day of our honeymoon, we drove to Memphis to close on our home and get the children. Yes, we took our children on the last three days of our honeymoon so that we could bond as a family.

Getting married, finding a home, and closing on it took fifteen days, but we did it. Everything was great for a while. After we were settled in our new home, we began to have frequent guests who felt like they did not to announce themselves. They just came when they felt like it. No deal—*wrong answer!* I would not have my home violated by anyone—especially people who were not saved. I had never allowed it, and I was not about to start.

Mind you, my husband had a wife who had died. In the three years he was single, raising his daughters, he said no one came over to help him, cook, clean, or even bring a meal. His eldest daughter only began reappearing when he and I were about to be married. I had to tell my husband to let her know that she could come over to our home whenever she felt like it. Once, I said that the war began.

When you have stepchildren—especially ones who are adults—you have to make sure that you put your foot down and take a stand. You and your mate have to sit down together and make sure that you have an understanding. You must make some ground rules without hiding the way you really feel. If you do not do this in the beginning, the enemy will definitely come in like a flood through people who are not saved or trying to be saved. With a blended family, everyone in the home has to know and understand that there are only two parents in the home. Everyone will come subject (follow the rules), including people who do not live in your home. If you do not, you will have some serious problems down the road.

When my husband finished talking to his eldest daughter—who, by the way, has her own family—she cursed, ranted, and wanted to know why she had to call. Remember, my husband is a pastor. He acted as if he was afraid to tell her to do those things out of respect, but he did. She continued acting silly, and then he yelled, "Where were you when the girls' mom—my wife—died? Why didn't you check on your sisters then? Why you wait till I got married to want to be a big sister?"

My stepdaughter said, "I don't have to come over here no d— more!" She got in her car and left. I knew that was not the last time that we would see her; I knew it (the situation) was not over.

I was a disciplinarian, and I taught my children to be responsible. My husband, on the other hand, worked a lot. He and his children went out to eat a lot, and he basically allowed them to do whatever they wanted. This was the total opposite of what he had told me in our conversation, but I found all these things out in the midst of confusion.

My children had to clean, cook if I worked late, do their homework right after school, go to bed on time, and go to church—I had rules to follow. My husband's children, on the other hand, did not have to clean, cook, or go to bed on time (unless they wanted to, not that he made them). They had no rules to follow, and he kept them out at all times of night at Wal-Mart.

After learning that there was a big difference in how my husband and I raised our children, I went to him and told him that we had to have a meeting of the minds ASAP. I knew that if we did not take care of our differences then, we would have some serious problems. I told my husband that his job was to take care of the home and family needs, and my job was to take care of the home, pay the bills, and care for children, which included setting ground rules. He was in total agreement—or so I thought.

As soon as one of his children was told no or that she could not do something, they would sneak and call my husband's eldest daughter. Suddenly, she would pop up unannounced, thinking she ran my home. She was wrong again. I got really tired and aggravated by the whole situation. I talked to my husband again, and he still could not see why it (her popping up unannounced) needed to be stopped. I explained to him that we were a family—he and I became one—and she needed to respect that as well as our home. We had eight minor children in our blended family to focus on—not his adult child.

My husband tried to talk to her (his eldest daughter) again, and she got very angry. She began manipulating the children and playing them against each other. I refused to tolerate this disruption in our home. She did not know me. I had to step in and cut off all communication until she got the picture and started acting like she had some sense. I had to remember what the Word said concerning my enemies.

Psalm 23:5 says, "Thou prepareth a table before me in the presence of mine enemies." Proverbs 16:7 says, "When a man's ways please the Lord, he maketh even his enemies to be at peace with him." After I was reminded of those words, I began dealing with her from a distance. I also had to remember that she was not saved or close to being saved.

Once she saw that I was the only woman running things in my home, she started calling first to see if she could come over. Although she did it in a childish manner, it did not matter; she called my husband and asked him. He either called me or told her she needed to call me—especially if I had plans that did not include extra people. Once these ground rules were established, we were on track, and our family began blending just fine without outside input or opinions.

With a blended family, you cannot treat children differently or allow anyone else to do so. I loved all my children the same. I never did anything for one I did not do for the other. My husband, on the other hand, went behind my back. He did things for one child and not the other, which brought about problems. I had to get him to see that.

God does not treat his children differently. His Word says he reigns over the just and the unjust. A blended family will never work if you are not truly walking as one. A house divided will not stand. As soon as our problems on the home front were settled, they started with the members at the church. The people of the church loved me—or so they said until my husband and I got married.

CHAPTER 6

TIRED, BROKEN, AND HURT IN THE CHURCH

Once my husband and I got married and I visited his church, I began to see a difference in some of the people. I said to myself, "There is no way I am going to leave my church and come over here." When you really want to make God laugh, tell him what you want and what you are not going to do. Truthfully, I would not advise you to do that unless you are ready for the consequences that will follow.

I thought that I would be able to stay at my own church and visit my husband's church every other Sunday or during special events. My pastor came to me and told me that even though he did not want me to go, I had to be with my husband, because he was the pastor, and it would not be right for us to be separated. I cried and cried. I did not want to leave, but it was a price I had to pay when I accepted the calling. I thank God every day for my trials and tribulation. This calling was just another test for a testimony. I could add to what God had already done in my life, so I stopped complaining and walked therein.

When I got there, I saw some things that needed to be done. I went to my husband and asked him about doing the work. I told him that I would pay for it myself, since I knew the church could not afford it. I thank God for my mom, because she came over to the church with me. God knew ahead of time I would need the support. When God gives you something to do, know that he already has people in place to support and give you what you need.

After the wallpapering, painting, and replacing blinds and curtains to beautify God's house, I thought the people of the church would be grateful that I was a worker and not someone who sat around, twiddling her thumbs. Some thought my work was nice, and others were negative, but I did not care. I did my work for the Lord, not them.

Women will always try to see how far they can push you when they cannot read you. I was definitely a person they (negative church members) could not read. Men do not have the insight that women have when it comes to other women. No matter how nice I was or how much love I showed, I still felt out of place. I felt the strong feelings of jealousy. They were used to doing things one way and did not understand that once the pastor got married, he could not take the whole church out to eat on Sundays. The church could not have his holidays anymore. I would not allow my family to be in bondage.

My children and I always celebrated our holidays as a family, and I could not sit back and let the holidays be taken away from us. There should be limitations as to how far a pastor goes with the members and his family. The first holiday that we had officially together before we were married was Labor Day; which was fine, because we were not married yet. I knew I was not going to let the church member's dictate how I spent my holidays.

You would think that when people say they love someone, they would have enough respect to allow that person to breathe. My husband could not breathe at all; the people were used to calling him for everything and at all times of the night. For some reason, they had a hard time setting boundaries after we got married. Of course, I did not have a hard time helping them. I tried to explain things to my husband about women and jealous spirits, but he was so hard-headed that I had to take him to the Word.

I took my husband straight to Proverbs 1:5–7: "A wise man will hear, and will increase learning; and a man of understanding shall attain unto wise counsel. The fear of the Lord is the beginning of knowledge: but fools despise wisdom and instruction." After reading the Word, all he could do was say, "I thought all my members were saved and sanctified."

I laughed and said, "Man, you should have some kind of insight. Their actions show you totally different." Although I continued to show nothing but love and respect, I only got it back from two members. Some women were jealous, because I did not act like they thought I should or act prissy. I only did things that should have already been done—what I was used to doing, which is being a servant. I continued to be mistreated, but I refused to allow my husband to continue to be used. I had to put a halt to it. God gave me my husband, and my job was to take care of what was mine.

God began to show me that some women desired to be me and wanted my husband. Once God allowed me to see various things, I felt that I had to go through some test that

I could not believe myself. One Sunday, during the after-service fellowship, I hugged everyone as usual. I walked to one woman to hug her, and she pushed my hands down and then pushed me in my back when I turned to walk away.

My natural man wanted to turn around and beat the crap out of her, but because I had allowed God to change, save, and sanctify me, I did not do anything. I told my children to come with me, because they were ready to fight. I dropped my children off, got in my car, went to the park, and cried like a baby. I wanted to know why God allowed that to happen to me when it took me seven years to be delivered from a fighting spirit and after all I had gone through with my husband's eldest daughter to stay saved.

I later began to realize that God was still molding me. God will allow you to go through storms, trials, and tribulations to mold you into what he wants you to be, not what you think you should be. Remember, every situation is only a test, and if you fail it, you will go through it again—worse than the first time. My children and I continued attending services, although they did not want to go there any more after that incident. I was not a parent who gave my children choices as to whether they wanted to go to church or not. I did not allow children to tell me.

Many parents have lost their way when it comes to rearing children. Children today tell the parent where they are and are not going, and that is very dangerous. If you fear your children or allow your children to dictate your actions, be prepared for all hell to break loose in your home.

I tried talking to my husband repeatedly about the things that I dealt with at the church and with the members, but he was so blinded by all the fake shouting and "hallelujahs" that he could not hear anything I said. It got to a point where I started to hate getting out of the bed on Sunday mornings. I knew that when I got complacent, something was definitely off. I got really tired of putting on fake smiles and pretending to be happy.

The situation continued to progress to the point that it started to affect our home and children. We argued all the time, and the children fought with each other, because my husband started sneaking around and treating the children differently, which brought about a division. I continued doing things the way they were supposed to be done, regardless of what he did. I knew that God would hold him accountable for his ways and actions, especially in the home. I told him that God would hold him accountable for the way he treated his family, and it only made things worse.

Things escalated to the point that my husband got up in the pulpit and put his family on blast, telling all our business. All of the children were angry. They did not want to sing in the choir, but he forced his biological children to sing. I refused to make my children continue suffering unnecessarily due to his lack of understanding and foolishness. God knows I loved my husband. I had already gotten tired, and he pushed me to a breaking point.

All of the children started to lose respect for my husband. They talked very disrespectfully to him. I stepped in and stopped all the drama but was persecuted by the members at the church for controlling my own home. Yes! My husband's children always ran to church members when I took away privileges or did not let them have their way. In turn, they ran to my husband, who would then come to me with hearsay.

I felt myself breaking, and it was not good. I would get into my vehicle and go to my secret place to pray. Do not allow the enemy to completely disrupt your home if you are a man or woman of God. Pray without ceasing. Listen to each other. Have a secret place to pray, and keep people out your business as well as your children's business.

I am a firm believer that parents should not argue in front of children. When my husband came home with his drama, I told him that he could say or call me whatever he wanted—just not in front of the children, because it would only create more confusion. He did argued anyway and had everyone in an uproar, including children, family, and church members. He continued to talk about our marriage, children, and problems in the pulpit until I completely broke one Sunday. I got my children and left.

As we walked out the door, he told us that if we walked out the door, we were some bastards. We left anyway. I could not take anymore. I decided that I would tell God about my husband and let God handle it. Sometimes it is better to just be quiet, pray, and allow God to fix your situation. Whatever your situation, it is not *bigger* than God!

By the time my husband realized that he was wrong, he had already hurt us and allowed most of the church members to treat us badly; with the exception of maybe three of the members. He apologized, and I forgave him, but he could never seem to put his foot down and keep it down. The woman at the church who pushed me had a fantasy in her mind that I took her place. She believed that she was supposed to be my husband's wife and the stepmom, so she continued to give me a hard time. I continued telling my husband, and again, denial sat in. He refused to believe that she wanted him, which kept the saga going on. She always wanted to know where we went and bribed his children so that they would tell her.

I was sick and tired of being sick and tired. I went to my husband's job to try to talk to him. Lo and behold, who did I see at his shop but this same woman? I called my husband over and told him she needed to stop coming to his shop. She needed to find another mechanic to work on her car, since she needed something fixed every week. Again, he brushed it off as if it were nothing, so we were back to square one.

I prayed and asked God if I really had to be hurt in the church. I could not take it anymore. I was not bothering anyone, so I did not want to be mistreated while my husband disregarded it. I was tired, broken, and hurt, and my soul grew weary. God knows how much we can bear. Just know that no matter what you are dealing with, he will not put more on you than you can bear.

Just as I was about to throw in the towel, God told me to move out of the way. I was in no position to move, because I did not have any money saved up, but the way was already made, and the transition was smooth. When God tells you to do something, do not look at your situation or circumstances, because the doors will open for you. God will back up his Word.

My husband was hurt. He cried and begged me to come home, but I had to be obedient. I was not about to get in God's way or interfere with His business, as many people try to do. My husband and I still talked every day; it was hard for me not to talk to him, because I loved him—flaws and all. Once I was away from his church, I was able to really allow God to heal me from the hurt I had encountered there. I had never been so hurt in a church before in my life; the healing was a long process.

If you have been hurt in the church, do not blame God or hold everyone accountable for small-minded people's ways. Remember that not everyone in the church is saved, so allow God to mend your broken heart and heal every wound that you have. Soar to the highest place God takes or is trying to take you in your life.

CHAPTER 7

GOING BACKWARD, AWAY FROM GOD, AND RESTORED

Just when I thought everything was all right, I started getting nasty phone calls from people saying crazy things to me. I ignored them and went on with my life. I continued to try to work on my marriage with my husband and me living separately. Things seemed to look up for us, because my husband began to open his eyes and really see what I had to endure while I was away from his church. My husband told me that he wanted me to come back home. I told him that God had to fix our situation, because he allowed the enemy to come in our relationship and destroy it.

My husband had let us get behind on all our bills, and our home was about to be foreclosed. I asked my husband how he let all these things happen and what he did with the money that I gave him for the bills. He went on to say that he owed some people, and his shop note was behind, which I did not understand. I told him I would not move back into the house, because he let too many people know where we lived. I am a private person. Every church member and almost every one of his customers knew where we lived, and that was not cool with me.

I went on to let my husband know that if he wanted his family back, he would have to find us another home. He agreed. One Saturday morning, my husband called and asked me out to breakfast. He said he had something to show and tell me. When we met at Shoney's, he told me that he had found a house and that he and the girls had already moved in. He wanted me to go see it after breakfast. He then went on to tell me that he has to get his life in order, because God had shown him his death if he did not. He seemed to be afraid of something. I asked him if everything was all right, and he said it was.

After breakfast at Shoney's , my husband and I went to the house. It was nice, but not as nice as the home we had. We made plans for him to come to my home later that evening to spend the night. I was excited, because it had been a while since we were together. Around 10:30 p.m., I had not heard from my husband. I called his phone repeatedly with no response. I just figured that a customer had called him, and he went to work on a car, like always.

This was one of our problems. Many times, we made plans, but business always came first. Do not allow things and business to come before your family. You never know what waits around the corner.

The next morning, I tried calling my husband again. There was no response, so I called his daughter's phone. She said he was not with her; she thought he was with me. I freaked out, because no one had heard from him. Then I thought that he may have worked on a car and fallen asleep at the shop. I got the children up to get dressed for church.

On our way to church, I called my husband's deacon to see if he was at church. The deacon said no. Then I began to worry. I asked the deacon to check the shop, since it was not far from his church.

When I finished talking to the deacon, I called the police to file a missing person's report. They tried to give me some crap about waiting twenty-four hours before they could file a report. I was not trying to hear, that we were talking about my husband; I went on to let them know that this was not normal for my husband, especially since the deacon told me that he was not at the shop. The operator went on to take down my husband's information. While she did that, I received another phone call stating that his eldest daughter went to our other home and found him dead.

I asked the operator to send the police to the house. I went into church, told my first lady what had happened, and left church to go to the house. Oh my God! When my family and I got there, people stared at me, called me names, and made false accusations against me. I was accused of killing my husband for some insurance money (which, to my knowledge, we did not have, because he had let everything get messed up).

I had never been more hurt or humiliated in my entire life. I had to go to the police station and be interrogated like a criminal. The officers said all the family members had to come in, because they always look at the spouse first and then the family. This was very stupid to me. Someone had killed my husband; I was questioned, threatened, and persecuted by people. The police did not even question the man who had threatened my husband; they did their own thing.

While the police gathered evidence, my husband's family went to his shop and the new house and stole everything. They even took the customer's car keys. I was so hurt and depressed that I could not even get out of bed. My first lady had to come over, get me up to go view the body, and make arrangements. I did not know where to begin or what to do. I was to the point of having a nervous breakdown, but she helped me keep it together.

When my children and I left my home on our way to the funeral home, I called the company my husband once had insurance with to see if they would cover my husband's funeral. To my knowledge, the policy was cancelled a couple months prior to his death. Well, to my surprise, he had cancelled it in 2007. All I could do was cry. After I hung the phone, my first lady said she knew someone who would work with me, which made me feel a little better. I did not want my husband buried in the county cemetery.

While my first lady and I were talking, my phone rang. The call was from another insurance agent who called to give his condolences and tell me that he needed me to come into his office to sign some papers. I asked him why, and he replied that my husband had a policy with his company. I wanted to know how and why, but before I could say anything, the agent told me that my husband did not want anyone to know about the policy, because if anything every happened, he did not want me to have to deal with his family (that was a joke to me) or have any needs.

My first lady and I both began to praise and magnify God. God knew that I could not afford the cost of a funeral. It was funny to me, because all the people who said they loved my husband—church members, family, and friends—none of them donated money or food for his funeral. They wanted to have a say in how I planned the funeral and wrote the obituaries. I started to be like them, but God would not let me. However, I let them put some names in the obituary, but I planned the funeral.

When day of the funeral came, everything went great until the burial. The insurance agent made it his business to go around and tell my husband's family that my husband had an insurance policy with me as the beneficiary, because he was trying to solicit customers for himself. When he did that, he started an uproar. People started talking and acting crazy, so again, I had to suffer persecution. I was devastated and hurt so badly that I did not even want to go to my husband's repast. My family told me not to worry about anything—that was my husband. I decided to go on and hold my head up in spite of the situation.

Once the repast was over, a young man who worked for my husband was cornered and threatened by the same man who had threatened my husband. This man told my husband's worker that he had better not open his mouth. When I found this out, I was upset that the police had their focus on the wrong person.

After everything was over, the insurance company called me and informed me that they could not pay out the money, because my husband's eldest daughter called them and said that I killed my husband. She had my stepchildren, my husband's church members, and even people in the jurisdiction believing that I had actually killed my husband. In spite of the talking and horrid looks, I continued to hold my head up. I went to church and refused to give in to their hatefulness. I did not once defend myself, because I was told to let God handle it. I took everything that was dished out, no matter how badly it hurt—and it really hurt.

I tried to go about my business, but people came at me as if I was some kind of villain. It got so bad that I had to let them know that I would not accept it anymore. I felt myself slipping away from God again, because I decided that if people wanted to come at me, they could. I would show them the old me. I wanted them to come at me; I was ready to beat somebody down. I wanted everybody who had said crazy things to me and thought I was afraid to approach me. I would not be a victim anymore.

I ended up having to get an attorney to fight the whole insurance issue. It took over two years before the case was even settled. I knew that God would fix everything. In the midst of all the drama, there were people who knew I had not done anything. I just wish they had come forth in the beginning instead of allowing me to suffer.

It became known that there was no possible way I knew about the policy. My husband had it in the church account, to which I had no access. My husband's successor called me and apologized for all I had to go through once he and his wife looked at the church finances. They saw that the policy had been in the church's account for a while and that the church was left in a financial bind.

I had forewarned the finance committee to take the finances away from my husband when God gave it to me. Everyone began to see things differently and realize that I only tried to help. It was too late; they had already pushed me to my limit. I had a lot of hatred in my heart for everyone who talked about me and looked at me as if I were crazy. I did not see myself ever forgiving any of them—even the leaders. These people caused me to have a nervous breakdown while I dealt with all this mess.

My friend and I went to a revival, and I was called out. I really did not want to go up there to the altar, but I thank God for an obedient spirit. The evangelist told me that the money that I had tied up was going to be loosed. Everyone who had put his or her mouth on me would suffer and have to come and repent to me. I felt the power of God overshadowing me. Tears ran down my face; my heart broke, and walls came down. God restored me—and I wanted restoration.

I allowed God to come in and restore me, and at the next court date, God released everything that was due to me. When the money was released, I did not even want it most of it. I gave it away, as God had directed me to. When you are in the midst of a storm and God speaks to the wind, hear his voice the first time. You can keep yourself from going through unnecessary storms. Do not allow the enemy to come in and consume you.

Let go of unforgiveness. Take your power back, and start living today. If you continue living with unforgiveness, you allow a person, situation, or thing to control who you are and what you become. A person who is dead can control your life if you do not forgive. Just know that everything you go through prepares you for something better. No matter what it seems like, God is right there beside you. You may not feel like God is there, but He is. No weapon formed against you shall prosper. God did not say the weapons would not be formed, He said they would not prosper.

Luke 19:8 says, "And Zacchaeus stood, and said unto the Lord; Behold, Lord, the half of my goods I give to the poor; and if I have taken anything from any man by false accusation, I restore him fourfold." Galatians 6:7–9 says,

> Be not deceived; God is not mocked: for whatsoever a man soweth, that shall he also reap. For he that soweth to his flesh shall of the flesh reap corruption; but he that soweth to the Spirit shall of the Spirit reap life everlasting. And let us not be weary in well doing: for in due season we shall reap, if we faint not.

Allow God to be your pilot, not the copilot, and watch how fast your storm passes over. Stand in the midst of all adversities, and watch God change things. You will be the head and not the tail. You will be the lender and not the borrower. Cast all yours cares upon him, for he cares for you.

Let God restore, lead, and guide you. Giving up is not an option, so hold on—help is on the way! You are victorious. Now, go take back everything the devil has stolen from you.

It's Not an Option

Born in poverty, deceit, hurt, and shame,

It took me a while to learn how to spell my own name.

Having a dream—never knowing what it would become,

I was desperate to be able to say in the end, I had won.

Giving up or quitting was not an option,

I had to continue to push and press.

Inside, I knew that one day, I could be the best.

I stopped wondering about my dreams and sitting around as though I were a mole.

I had to get up and make something happen if I wanted to reach my goal.

Giving up or quitting was not an option.

Now that I've grown, pushed, and pressed, my determination and drive have made me the best.

So giving up, quitting, or just stopping are not options.

Bring your dreams and goals to life, no matter where you come from—everything else is not an option.

CPSIA information can be obtained at www.ICGtesting.com
Printed in the USA
LVOW110055200412

278390LV00001B/7/P